GAYLE HEIMBACH BRADSHAW

Gayle Heimbach Bradshaw

Hope Through the Fire

Outskirts Press, Inc.
Denver, Colorado

ACKNOWLEDGEMENTS

To my son, David, whose smile always lights up my heart and fills my life with love.

To my sister, Donna, and my friend, Carl, for being the best friends I've ever known.

Thanks to Steve, Ronnie, and Crafton for being true friends and always being there.

Thanks to Scott and Eric for reminding me it is okay to laugh.

Thanks to my mother, Betty Heimbach, and to Steve Cunningham for helping me put the book together. And thanks to my mother for encouraging my writing from the time I was very young, and always keeping me in her prayers. Love ya, Mom.

To my sister, Leslie, for helping me manage day-to-day affairs, and inspiring me to push on.

To my brother, Darryll, with fond memories of BB guns and basketball.

To my father, Ray, for our growing friendship.

Thanks to my doctors and counselors over the years:

Dr. Hansel, Dr. Hunt, Dr. Rubenstein, Carol, Dr. Shaurette, Dr. Wallace, Chaplain Myers, Dr. Burch, Ms. Christian, Chaplain King, Rev. Ferguson, Ms. Grant, Dr. Voris, Ms.B. Hanna, Ms. Mazza and Ms. Jenkins.

Thanks to Chaplain Myers for his prayers, and for always pointing me to the Lord.

In memory of

Dr. Shaurette, misunderstood by many, but to those of us who knew him he was a blessing to our world.

HOPE

Sometimes reaching for hope
Is like reaching for a blade of grass
In a blaze of fire
You may get burned
You may want more time
For old wounds to heal
But you must reach in
And grasp the hope
And go on

INTRODUCTION

Living with schizophrenia and depression is a journey. It is both frustrating and frightening. I may not know all the answers, but through my poems, I hope I will be able to help you find encouragement. This book is about the life of war I experience every single day. It is about the results of abuse. This is a book about hope...and it is applicable to anyone's struggles.

Many of the poems speak of despair, others of joy. I have found strength and comfort in Almighty God. He has helped me through many overwhelmingly desperate moments. I pray that as you read these poems, they will be a catalyst toward wholeness. At times, it can help just to know that someone else knows exactly how you feel...and that they made it through it. It has been said, "Sometimes the only way out of a situation is through it." I pray that no matter what we must face from day to day, we can have..."Hope Through The Fire".

CONTENTS

BOUND

Tiptoeing the tightrope of sanity
Afraid to live, and afraid to die
Afraid to quit, and afraid to try
The pit and the mountain,
they beckon and call
I step toward the mountain
slippery and tall--glancing back
The great chasm with its trials of fire,
I grasp the cool rock
and try to pull a step higher
Ropes bind my form to the depths below
where failures and fears
line its smoldering glow
Each move I make,
the bonds restrain me yet more
Time rages…
and roars.
I attempt with all my might
to somehow break free,
and puzzle together
what used to be me
Afraid to live--and afraid to die
Afraid to quit--and afraid to try

GAYLE HEIMBACH BRADSHAW

A PRAYER FOR FAITH

I've been learning to cry again,
for I'd forgotten how.
Learning how to live with myself,
to live in the here and now.
I want to be a real person
out of the torturous grip of my past.
Flashbacks, memories . . .
It all comes so very fast.
I'm so afraid
My heart feels it will burst.
Inner pain and confusion
I'm not sure which came first.
Where do I go from here?

I don't want to be afraid anymore
and I have been for so very long.
How do I change the ingrained beliefs?
How do I become strong?
I want to believe there's good ahead.
I want to believe there's life in store.
How can I keep
the life I sometimes feel?
When everything gets confused,
and I'm not sure what's real.

My heart aches deep within,
as though I've not faith enough,
But I want so much to be brave and strong
and I want so much to be loved.

HOPE THROUGH THE FIRE

Hope is hard to feel some moments,
when there's confusion, and desperation,
and you want to walk away from it all.
You wander through empty corridors,
hoping someone will hear your call .
So, I pray I've something to give--
Something to give from inside
Anything that will make my being here
Something different than if I died.

Understanding escapes me.
Why have things happened as they have?
The hurt in my heart
makes me tired and makes me sad.

I cannot see tomorrow,
I cannot see this eve.
But I know I must hold on—
I know I must believe.

Give me strength, my God,
and faith to make it through
With the passing of each moment,
Help me to know what's true.

Grant me hope, dear Lord.
Send friends to fuel the flame.
Brightly burn the heat of love
'til I am nevermore the same.

Help me to believe—

To take new steps with each day.
Teach me hope through the fire—
And faith along the way.

BRACE

Sitting here in the darkness…
There's so much I do not know
I feel I'm in a prison…
Is there much pain left to go?
I glance outside my window
No light breaks through the night
I hold my breath and pray
My muscles drawn so tight
Brace against impulse
Brace against time
Brace against your own heart—
For they say my bloodshed is a crime
When will the torture end?
..and the shadows fade away…
when will the terror in my mind
find words enough to say
I cannot tell of the horror
Just to hear someone call my name
…I try to hide inside…
but each time it's the same
Don't look at me
Your eyes pierce me like a knife—
Running through the shame—
The disgust of my whole life
I stumble around the shrouded mines
…my spirit's last decay
as I pray to God Almighty
please.. help me find the way

FRIENDSHIP

Some friendships are like a rose—
Beautiful at first, but soon die off
Others are like a dying bud—
They never really become much of anything
There are friendships like grass—
They last for a season
But true friendships are like an evergreen—
Beautiful and growing year 'round

PRESSURE

There's an incapacitating weight
Pushing against my mind
Pressure builds and builds
And I'm standing on a line.
I strive to keep control—
I don't even know what's on the other side.
But I fight against it with all I've got,
Looking for reasons I just can't find.
My thoughts are all scrambled,
I can't look at one alone.
They evade my grasp and take away
The little insight that I've known.
I hold tightly to the hand of God
Knowing this moment will pass
And that moments of joy and inspiration
…those are the memories that last

In this poem, help arrives in time. Unfortunately, in life that is not always true. When battling suicidal thoughts or thoughts of self-harm, it is important to hold on to God and other people. In my own life, I have found a couple of things that help me to stay safe. For me it helps to try not to allow suicide as an option. I know, it sounds a lot easier than it really is. You can't choose what thoughts come into your mind—but you do choose what you do with those thoughts. The other thing is to TALK to someone—anyone—and don't quit until you find someone who is really listening sincerely, and non-judgmentally. There are people who do care. So, if you are struggling with self-destructive thoughts, don't quit until you have found someone. Don't stop. God brought me through many suicide attempts. I don't know why He did…but I am so glad now. Keep the faith!

THE RECORD STOPPED

Sunstreams pierced the darkness
Plagal, icy sheets crudely glazed the window, and
the light drifted, down to the room below.
A young woman crouched in the corner
She sat there—holding her head,
Hoarsely whispering, her reasoning dead

The phonograph churned—
"Sunshine, on my shoulder
makes me "happy—happy-happy"
Her hands dripped sweat
On the cold steel handle
Her freezing arm was wet
Both hands were on the knife
Each fought for control
One pitted against the other,
As desperation took its toll.
Her eyes were glazed, but mobile
Darting wildly in her craze
Her pale hands shook in rhythm
As she fought against the rage
Pressure built inside her head
On and on toward explosion
The overwhelming ache inside
The catalystic one
Pain shot through her chest
Driving vision from her eyes
And the ghoulish face of death
Began to peel off its disguise

As her heart could bear no more
She cried out in despair
Dropping the weapon
She sank to the floor

She wiped at the tears
Now streaming down her face
…gasping for air
from what seemed an endless race
Sitting in her vomit and stench
She heard glass crunch
And two people knelt beside her
And took her hands in love
They placed their arms around her
Lifting her to her feet
A new chance at life
In her world full of pain, regrets, and defeat

As they left the old tomb,
The record stopped…
And the "rest" began.

ONCE A MARINE

Army, Navy, Air Force, Marines
With something deep inside,
we transcend ordinary means.
Something in the heart –something in the soul
A commitment deep within
that somehow makes us whole.
A drive deep inside
most don't understand.
Devotion to our country--
like touching God's own hand.
A purpose before unknown –
difficult to express,
A longing to make a difference
In a world of conflict
And unrest
Sometimes we face choices
The gray between right and wrong
Trying to balance oaths and hearts
Only makes us more strong
Having a chance to make a difference
….well that's the chance of a lifetime
And the goals we had set for ourselves
We find ourselves surpassing those lines
Dedication to our country
Which we have served so well
Births a sense of honor
Words can never tell

NONE HAVE SEEN

Where is the life
of which I dreamt so long ago?
Little stick figures are sprinkling tears
on yesterday's fallen rainbow
My heart aches and bleeds
over the "me" that none have seen.
There is so much inside.
I have so much to give,
but no one to accept it
in this world in which I live.
And, in this world,
down is up - and up is down
My mouth can cry for help,
but my hands and feet are bound.
A maze of walls and halls
steps that lead nowhere
Turning corners – walking into glass--
I fight the devil's dare.
My heart aches and bleeds
Over the "me" none have seen

LUMINOUS GLORY

Luminous glory of a summer night
silently, splendidly
fills the sky with all of God's majesty
Mysteries untold
and an unfathomable Creator
Sweetly showers peace
upon those below
The Son's divine blessing
brings awe and wonder
Daybreak
comes with the morning dew
kiss of a rose
Oceans raise their hands
Mountains stand and sing
For Divine God
brings another chance for life,
blossoming with Joy

INTRODUCTION TO POEM
" IN THE MIDST"

Stationed overseas in the Marine Corps, I loved life, and thought myself to be invincible. One night as I walked from my apartment to base, I met up with a gang. I never once considered that the events of that day would change my life forever—yet they did. The gang attacked and raped me, and I have never been the same again.

The attack brought flashbacks not only of that horrible night, but also of sexual abuse I went through growing up.

I've asked myself and asked myself if I could have foreseen or prevented the attack. I don't know the answer. Was there another route I could have taken? If I had left 10 minutes earlier or later would I have avoided being in the wrong place at the wrong time? Was it simply poor judgment, and therefore justified? I don't know.

I still don't have the answers. But I also know I can't spend my life trying to find answers or reasonable explanations. I can't live *today* if I'm consumed with the past and all the "what-ifs." I'm learning daily to focus on this moment. I have *now,* the present, and want to make the most of it. Thanks to the mercy and grace of a loving God, I have begun to let go of regrets, shame and recriminations…while reaching out to take hold of a new hope for the future and my growing faith in the Almighty.

IN THE MIDST

I feel it
I feel them—touching me
Faces looms threatening
I try hard not to see
Unspeakable things they do
And it kills my heart inside
My body consumed in terror
No sense or awareness of time
Separate from the horror
I let my body die
Keeping my eyes fixed on the sky,
I simply hide
My body is dying, yes
To no feeling at all
Just waiting for it to be over
I scream inside—God hear my call!
Why all this?
I don't understand
But somehow through the silent tears
I feel God take my hand
And I try hard not to cry
But I know when this is over,
He will help me stand

HIDE

Take me away—as fast as you can
Hide the light of day.
Run, run girl,
No place forever to stay.
You belong nowhere
None belong to you
No one sees your heart
No one knows the truth
Truth? Reality?
Hide. Hide. Hide.
I cannot take much more
Is this all I'm living for?
I cannot close my eyes
There's too much inside to see.
Tomorrow—No more sorrow
If they will just let me be.

IN PRAISE

God,
I long for Your presence.
What a joy…. to be by Your side.
I delight to come before You,
surrendering the thoughts of my mind.
May I sing Your praises forever,
as I bow before You now.
I pledge my days to serve You,
my hand is to the plow.
Nothing brings more joy
than singing to Your name.
I delight in Your love
and I'll never be the same.

NO END IN SIGHT

When emotions are running high
and impulse is the name of the game,
the only thing you know for sure
is you have yourself to blame.
Destructive drive comes and goes
in an overwhelming tide
You want to scream and run from it,
but there is no place to hide.

You're running from yourself
But she won't let you off--
That little girl inside
who wants so much to talk.
But as soon as she comes close
desperation rules in power
and that rumbling destructive train
pulls you on another hour.

The wind is blowing strongly,
and you're on the tightrope again--
Never really knowing
if this time you'll meet your end.
A million times a week,
you tell the world goodbye
But hell goes on inside,
…with everything you try.
Then when the battle's over,
you're on a shocking high
that refreshes you

and somehow makes you glad you didn't die.

How do I get down to
what brings the gripping pain?
That desperation that does not change,
yet is never twice the same.
I cannot stop these cycles,
though I try with all my might.
Up and down and up and down
There is no end in sight.

But then, sight is not the end
I've been blessed enough to learn
After the struggle I sometimes fear
Pain eases as though break of dawn
And, I know,
It's those moments that I fear will not change
That are actually catalysts toward strength
Learning to hold tightly
Knowing the light will soon break through the rain

NO MORE DUES

Tiptoeing through the maze
of my confused and crazed beliefs,
trying to find direction
in these fogged and darkened streets
How did I get here?
and how do I break free?
How do I return to
the grace I once received?
I fight so not to sacrifice
from that relentless drive to pay
It almost seems impossible
to be forgiven when I pray
It must be something else,
my efforts I struggle to defend
my desire to offer penance
for myself and for my friends
   show my God I'll do anything,
   any price I have to pay,
    if only He will see my heart
   and hear me when I pray
Only His light can heal
my poison-riddled mind,
that the debt of my redemption
somehow must be mine
It would be easier to believe
if I could just endure the pain,
    if I could hurt enough,
   the guilt would finally wane
I work with all my might

but I simply can't erase
the unclean, withered spirit
of long-soured, bitter taste
How can I let it go?
I know I somehow must
    but I do not understand His word
    I need the Master's touch
What is the reality of the cross?
That He'll forgive me of my sin?
Will heal my constant terror?
When can I receive--when?
When does it count for me?
He died for me
Is that really true?
    My stained, defiled spirit--
    can He make this life brand new?
How do I believe?
How do I release to you
this painful, endless need?
Dear God, my heart longs for you
more each moment of the day
where lack of faith has grown
into so many shades of gray
God, work inside my heart
break down the hidden walls
that house the deafening silence
of these cold and lonely halls

Have mercy on my soul,
I hear you sweetly call.
I surrender now with everything,

the doubts, and fears and all
Forgive me, Lord, the ugliness,
the hideous, loathsome sins
Cleanse my spirit—renew my soul
Let's begin again
Your precious, precious love
heals me as I dream,
It fills my inner thirst
with soft, and gentle streams
    Let your Spirit be reborn in me
    as you wash it all way
    Joy cascades into my heart
    for I no longer have to pay

CURRENTS OF LOVE

Life is a flowing brook
sometimes bubbling, sometimes rushing on
and though it feels a trickle today
I see a new day has begun.
The currents I cannot control,
but handle them as I may
Starting over again and again,
to each a brand new day.
Where will it take me this morn?
Can I leave my sorrow behind
and float on the love of my Lord?
Are there new joys and truths to find?
I step forward into the stream,
wading, trying to find my way.
I slip into the stream tenderly
Carried along, I surrender and pray
A new day

ALL OR NOTHING

It's all or nothing, God
I can't stand to live in compromise
Claiming Your name, but doing my will
Hurting You so, yet loving You still
When I fail I wish I could die,
And only a touch from You
Can make me try—again
If I'm going to keep on failing,
And never really grow
I'd rather die right now
Than not live the things I know
But if I'm going to make it,
If I'm really going to change,
Please give me faith now
Take my thoughts and rearrange

It seems my life is hopeless
Without Your peace in my heart
Wake up my zeal for You
That I had back at the start
Help me when I fail
Not to feel so bad that I just do more
But to trust it to You, get up, forget it
And remember that's what You died for
I want to be almost fanatic in sharing You
And living in Your love
The way You want me to

Lord, it's all or nothing
Let's try for all

INNOCENCE LOST

Since----ever so little
There has been no place to hide
Stripped of my body
Stripped of my pride
As I grew
Violated again and again
all I've ever known

My adult life
Has been much the same
Raped and left
Feeling I'm the one to blame
When does it end?
Will I ever trust again?
I've nothing left
With which to defend
I feel naked
Even when I'm fully clothed
I look in the mirror
My own face I loathe
Do you hear my cry, Jesus
Won't you throw me a line?
My body has been so used
It seems it's never been mine
I give this scarred body to you
I pray for your strength
And I pray one day…
You'll give me back my innocence

BIRTH

I don't really understand
This place I'm in
Fighting against
All I've ever been
Moving from being a victim
To a brand new world
It's as though I'm in labor
Looking at upcoming hidden turns
Which do I take?
I make ready my heart
For I know not where I'm heading
But I know I've made a start
The labor brings life
I control my breaths as best I can
I know deep within
I am in God's strong hands
I must admit,
I'm a little bit cautious
It is beginning to seem
It's going to take a lot of trust
The fear that fuels my thoughts
And tries to dissuade the hope of my heart
--that fear is losing the battle
the cords of confusion are coming apart

SO UNCERTAIN

Do I have the right to laugh?
Do I have the right to smile?
It's so confusing
I'm uncertain all the while.
I feel I don't deserve
anything good from those around.
The raging thunder hits my heart
with a frightening, deafening sound.
I know God still cares
and I know why Jesus died
but, at times when Satan stalks me
I find no place to hide.
I know I should feel safe
in God's commanding, Almighty power
But confusion and fear
grow stronger with each hour.
Then, my mind gets slammed again
No concept of my future,
No understanding of where I've been.
I know that God has the power to change
my mind, my spirit, my will.
I continually come to Him
So why am I desperate still?

DEAD AND RISEN

Sitting quietly in the stillness of night
Easter morning just hours away
Praying my new commitment
Will take root before break of day
I silently scream within
For I am the reason He died
All the words fade away
As I see Jesus crucified
My heart is filled with horror
At the ghastly blood that flowed
How He endured such torture
I will never know
The jeers, the pain, the whole world's shame
How must have felt?
More difficult to bear
Than words can ever tell

Why would He go through such hell?
I should be upon the tree
I'll probably never understand
But that through it He set me free
My corrupt mind fights against His word
My spirit is so defiled
I cry and long for my Lord
As I walk this "surrender " mile
Here, today, I go back to the day
When he became the sacrifice for me
The day He paid the price
To heal each hurt and meet each need

HOPE THROUGH THE FIRE

I know I can never fathom
All He did to bring me life

I bring my sin to Him
The old nature now will die
I give my Father everything
All that is within…
My heart, my mind, my spirit, and soul…
Where I'm going and where I've been
I wish I could help God's heart to mend
From all the pain I've put Him through
I know that I have hurt Him
But I commit my heart anew
When Jesus died on the Cross
He lived my fears and He lived my shame
And there they've died with Him
And I will never be the same

Today, I celebrate his resurrection
The life beyond human death
A spring of hope and peace
More joy with each new breath
I am alive! Praise God I'm alive!
I live in Him and He lives in me
I look forward with sincere joy
To all that this day can be

Morning has come
I receive, from Him, His risen life
Dawn brings rebirth of my heart
A precious and glorious new sight

MORNING LIGHT

Last night seemed endless,
the confusion difficult to bear
Fear grew
into a living nightmare
But I know you are there--
I knew deep inside.
When terror struck
I came to You to hide
Morning is breaking,
I feel Your mercy
and come alive in You.
When things get so rough
and I cannot feel Your peace,
You remind me You control the winds
and the storm begins to cease

LOST TRACK

I lost track of You for a while there, God
Where did You go?
I could not speak Your name,
though I've tried everything I know.
I couldn't pray,
A wall of fire has kept us apart.
I feel so very alone
Feels like I've lost my heart.
Did You leave me, Lord?
It seems whatever I do
You choose to ignore.
Can I count on You?
Do You know my name?
These demons tried to steal You from me
But I've held tight 'til You came.
I know Your words,
they take me through the night
and at high noon
they give me fuel to fight.

JOY UNEXPECTED

God what has happened?
My Lord, what have you done?
My God,
Is it true that you love me?
That you care about my mind,
About what I hear and see?
I've come to you so many times
And humbly surrendered all
But then verses and voices become twisted
And I think it is your call
I'm told you would not ask of me
All I think You are
I leap forward in belief
But then, I stumble far
I know when I try to explain
Myself to those around
They do not know my heart
Words tiptoe around
But I know today you see,
See all that is within
My fears, my dreams
And where my spirit has been
If you care, Jesus
If you really do
That's all that matters to me
Make me all you want me to be
And when demons come
Or chemicals rage
Help me know how to believe in you

HOPE THROUGH THE FIRE

Help me out of their torturous cage
I put my trust—right now—in You
Let this be a fresh start
Of a life I can hold onto.

TWIRL INTO HEAVEN

Twirling, swirling,
fueled by the soft, subtle breezes of fall
Leaves flutter about
as though moved by the Master's call.
The change of season
eases into our hearts
Where all true hope and rest
seem to have their start.
Water ebbs and flows,
gently upon the shores.
Mountains are shadowed by heavenly hues,
right up to heaven's front door.

OBEY HIS WORD

When you love enough
 to sacrifice your dreams,
to follow the call
and all that can mean.
A heart that is ready,
with all its might,
To do what God commands
To do what is right.
When I cannot see,
I simply look above
Praising and worshiping
in power and love.
Obeying for His grace
Obeying yet His will
Some question God's words,
But He is with me still

BLESSED

They say all good things come from you, God
So how did I rate this?
Peace I never dreamed of ..
So much of life I've missed.
I don't know why You decided to bless me,
But it joys my very soul.
Living in Your love, serving You,
Lord, my utmost goals.
There has been so much confusion over the years.
There's a lot I don't understand,
Not a single thing
Has gone the way I planned.
I quit planning a long time ago.
I found it only brought pain
To my heart and to my soul.
I'm trusting my all to You
In a brand-new start.
Somehow, some way,
You revived my very heart.
I don't feel like I deserve it,
But I'm letting that go.
You love, and You care…
That's all I need to know.
You're such a wonderful God.
How can I say thanks?
Let my service speak it to Your heart
I thought my soul would never wake.
I commit my life to You
I want so much to show You my love

I long to live as You wish,
Holy life anew
The beginning of all I've never known.

ON THE LINE

Whirling, swirling
My mind and heart on the line
With all of God's promises
His love and His grace
Why does peace seem so hard to find?
How many times have I come to place...
Where my heart fails me
and I feel my life's a waste
Do I choose to believe the good
With all my being
Though my courage fails me
I step forward with confused feelings
So here it is…
Do I trust what I cannot see?
Does the Almighty see my pain?
Does He see my need?
I will believe
I will believe
I come, Lord,
My soul and mind I bring
Please heal all the ageless pain
And cause my heart to sing

CURRENTS OF LOVE

Life is a flowing brook
sometimes bubbling, sometimes rushing on
and though it feels a trickle today
I see a new day has begun.
The currents I cannot control,
but handle them as I may
Starting over again and again,
to each a brand new day.
Where will it take me this morn?
Can I leave my sorrow behind
and float on the love of my Lord?
Are there new joys and truths to find?
I step forward into the stream,
wading, trying to find my way.
I slip into the stream tenderly
Carried along, I surrender and pray
A new day

CAPTIVE HEART

My God,
I'm searching for truth
Searching for hope
as the soft, silent moon appears
I can't be sure of anything
Is it night?
Is it day?
Does it matter anyway?
For the deep, dark abyss swallows me whole
I struggle for a foothold,
But the cool, earthen walls crumble away--
leaving me buried in the soil

And as the walls become wider,
the hole stretches yet more
I'm searching for a way out
away from the pain and torture
I pray to You to show me the way,
As I struggle for just one more day
One more day, one more chance for life
But courage evades me as the walls of my life
fall before me--around me--through me

A PRAYER IN DESPERATION

Dear God,
When I feel this confused and desperate,
I come to you
with all I am, and all I feel
It's a time when reason is difficult
and death seems close and real
My heart cramps, and my body jerks,
and I feel at a total loss
So, I come to you to draw from
the very power of the Cross

That power alone can take me through
a morning of darkest hell,
and bring me hope and victory
from your precious, living well.
Make me strong, Lord
Heal these bones
That wax cold, and brittle and weak
As I come to You wholeheartedly
Give me strength for all I must meet

JUST DON'T KNOW

I don't know how
I don't know why
But the very thought of Your love
makes me laugh and makes me cry.
I want so much to serve You
but I'm out here on a limb.
Help me down, Dear God,
Catch me if You can
For the ground below me
is overgrown with seeds of doubt
A barren, dry place
Lord Jesus, I want out
Can't You stop this pain?
Can't You heal my heart?
The visions and the voices
are ripping me apart
Why do You stand afar now?
when I need You so very much
I know I don't always remember
what to do to feel Your touch
Don't You care at all, Lord?
Don't You want to help?
I'm looking for Your presence,
But it's like I'm by myself
Please bring to me fresh hope
For I know there is more than this
I know there is joy in You
It is Your love and grace that I miss
I'm letting go

Put my feet on solid ground
Strong and firm
No longer bound

SO SUNNY SUNDAY

It's now a sunny Sunday afternoon
The rain has stopped and there is
a gentle freshness in the air
Children prance around the parking lot
with their Barbie dolls and their raceway cars

From my balcony, I see them
But the children do not seem to notice
They play as all children do
And pretend
Cowboys and Indians
Playing house
Roller-blading between the cars

Geese come over from the lake,
their smooth, rounded bodies waddling along

And for the first time in a long time,
as I watch these scenes,
I do not feel alone
Even if there is no one for me to talk to
I feel a part of the larger scheme
And I know I must find
my place in this world,
just as those I survey

LONELY HEART

I own a lonely heart,
I come and lay it down.
This panicky insecurity
Lord, turn it all around..
Help me to find peace and love,
in Your everlasting arms.
Ease the fear of myself,
as You shield my heart from harm.
Help me to feel as comfortable
with just You and me,
To not needs others around
just to be what I should be.
Let my "me" be in You,
Sitting quietly in this cool breeze.
I come to You, dear Jesus,
To heal each hurt and meet each need.
Take this lonely heart, Dear God,
I surrender it all to You.
Help me to walk in this life,
Every day anew.

Two of the horrors of my illness are visions, and
voices…a time when night and fear go hand-in-
hand. It's something I never dreamt of in my "Jesus
Loves Me" world. God is my only comfort. Some
moments it is so scary I feel like I just got dropped
into the middle of hell.

SHADOWS

Shadows fall
The air reeks with decay
An enormous hairy hand
Greenish and molten gray
Reaches through the bars
Touching me on the shoulder
As if he had a right
A God-given right to be there
Cords of confusion twist and turn
Like eels within my head
They tell me I must sacrifice
To do what the Lord said
Staggering on the line
of life and insanity
Fear coursing though my veins
The hellish truth that is me

EVERY BREATH

The eerie smell
The shadows
In the corner
The baby demons doze
The devil himself
Is haunting my every breath
I cannot find myself
Lord, is this some test?
Jesus, take me home
If that is what it takes
To stop my endless torture
Morning, noon and night
Help me

SO FAST

What is this coming against me?
Lord, where are you now?
I' m so very afraid.
Where is Faith?
By now I should know how.
Please hold my hand,
Ease the ache inside.
Please help me bring to you
these fears I try to hide.
Why don't I feel stronger?
Do you still love me, Lord?
Just days ago I felt so free.
Why does it change so fast?
It only seems a few hours
Yesterday has passed.
Five minutes at a time...
What was it like five minutes ago?
So much, so much fear
My heart is trembling so
How do I turn this around?
Bring me faith and hope
Sort through the confusion
Help me live the things I know
I still my thoughts
And place my hand in Yours
I know You are truth
And will reign in my heart forevermore

WHISPERING LIGHT

The sun splashes down
Where there was no light
Chasing demons from the corners
What terrifies at night
Becomes more safe, more familiar
With the long-awaited break of day
Dead leaves flutter about
My dog barks at these
And chases them until they are lost
In the leaf-combed brown grass of winter
The chirping of birds
The tingling of chimes
What a wonderful place to be
Here, in the sun
My dog (and friend) Sherlock
Demands his share of attention
His coat so soft and warm
The clarity of the sun
Brings an almost drugging effect
In the brilliance of the sunlight
I know God is near
I cannot see nor hear Him
But I know it is He
That is whispering in the soft breeze
And in the surety of the light

GOD LOVES ME

When I hear those words
The walls begin to crumble away
Layer by layer the darkness is broken
And the tomb is etched by rays of day
My heart has been chained
By my own mind
Struggling for what is real
Words cannot express my heart
Can't shout the joy I feel
Wow, Lord.
To think you actually love me
I've always been afraid if I believe
It would be snatched before I could see
Now I know Your power cannot be conquered
My heart leaps within me
The most incredible thing I've ever known
The Almighty thinks of me
Another piece falls into place
And the border of my vision
Melts from leather into lace

LORD HEAL MY MIND

Here we are again
It seems the battle never ends,
this desperation that rages in my soul
Change the drive, bring new life
Somehow make me whole
This confusion frustrates me so...
The twisted hearing of your voice
When I battle to believe Your Word
help me make the choice
It seems I hear You speaking,
But it simply makes no sense
The voices and visions
Leave me straddling the fence

I struggle against principalities,
against all hell itself
I pray that you will heal my mind,
that you will make me well.
There is an illness, yes I know,
but spiritual war as well.
All together it maims my spirit
as words can never tell.
Please, heal distortions, my very thoughts
Correct even the chemicals inside
Bring to me the peace of mind
I ever long to find

Rejuvenate my body
Bring the stability I crave so much.

My efforts alone can't change a thing,
Lord, I need your touch
Here, I surrender my heart
I surrender all my fear.
Please hear my cries to you--
bring hope to dry the tears

IN FLIGHT

Fly
I'm gonna fly away
....my heart unleashed
Oh, a brand new day
I'm soaring
High above in the glistening blue
Pinch me, I'm dreaming
Can this freedom be true?
My heart is open
My arms wide apart
I embrace my Savior
What a glorious start
So elementary...
Why so long to understand?
I'll skip and twirl and run
....the Lord said I can....

IN HIS STEPS

Stepping gently into His footprints,
Haven't spent much time in supposition.
Maybe just a little nervous, that's all.
I think I'll inch a step closer
I'm not sure where this will take me...
I've just scaled another wall.

Can He tell me,
Or is this part of being free?

Where I go from here
Is a choice He left to me.
I love Him enough to march on,
Should it matter that I can't see?
I long for him to know the immeasurable love
That carries me through the fear,
The love that resounds from within
Simply because my Lord is here.

WITHOUT A HOME

Homelessness is a horrible failure of our society
Where frustrated, scary lives drone on
Few to walk with, few to talk with
Nothing to call their own
"A nuisance" the blessed
would rather not deal with
mitigating circumstances
they blindly miss

Such loneliness
Eats at the very core
Until one feels his soul will die
And he won't feel anymore
Not feel peace, nor despair
Not feel anything at all
It's a prison without walls
They cry out to Almighty God
And wonder why this world does not understand
Doesn't remember that
Though they may be without a home
They are never without a heart
Confused, afraid
Afraid of so very much
Society's victims again
Swallow the lump in their throat and walk on

IN THE DARKNESS

Awake in the dark—
Awake in the dark
Terror—fear of demons
Have left their mark.
So, so afraid
My heart feels it will burst
Inner torture, confusion, fear
I'm not sure which came first.
Hold me, dear Jesus.
Please ease the pain inside.
You alone know my heart's wars…
You alone hear my cry.
So much I don't understand
Not always sure my life is real.
So much confusion
I'm not sure what I'm supposed to feel.
Trust who? Believe who?
Visions of those I love most
Clearly plot my destruction
Then gather to laugh and boast
Each and every day
Is another frightening test
The demons are after me
With a new and refueled zest.

WITHIN THIS HELL

Where are You, God?
In this hell I'm in?
I feel like I'm drowning
Please, not this again
If You're here with me,
Won't You take my hand?
My knees are giving way
I need your help to stand
I'm so very afraid , Dear Lord
I can't see my next step
The road's a mushy, clouded stream
From the tears that I have wept
They say You count our tears…
Have You time to count when I cry out?
…When I cry out for You, dear God?
My mind is shattered by fears and doubts,
And my heart is broken
Why do you want me here?
Why don't You love me Lord?
Like those in Your Word You hold so dear?
What is it I have done?
So much confusion, and such shame
I remember long ago You loved me
I loved to sing Your praise,
But now when I praise, there's nothing
Why can't You love me the same?
I give it all to You, Lord,
Here I am, my heart is open
Please fill it with Your love

Please Lord, please tell me
I need not shed more blood
Heal my mind
Please heal my soul
If these demons don't leave soon.
I fear my mind will go

AN AMERICAN ON 9/11

What can I say of this country of mine?
How can I express the flame within?
In the desperation of the attack, all hands joined,
We'll never be the same again.
Passion burns brightly,
love of country and each other,
the sometimes silliness of another.
All the little things we may have taken for granted
are all the things for which we stand.
Freedom to speak, Freedom of religion,
Freedom to pursue our dreams...
Freedom in ways other countries
to this day have never seen.

Americans are special--
It's something basic in the heart.
A man's hope to become all he longs to be,
no matter where his start.
What now?
Its fear can grip as a vise
But we step forward as we meet each day
ready to pay the price.
Many paid it before, and now we face the challenge.
There is much we must sacrifice.
At moments we all must pause,
To kneel before God, to cry.
Then strengthened to meet .
A blaze of passion in each heart and hand.
Praise God, to be an American

Our heart hearts stand—-our voices sing.
To be an American--
What an amazing thing.

CHANGE OF SEASON

I've gone through a long winter in my heart
Now it's finally Spring
New life blossoms inside,
and I find myself beginning to sing.
Singing of the joy and peace
God has brought to me
It's more than overwhelming
More than I thought life could be!

The winter has melted in my soul.
It is time to celebrate life.
A gentle rain softly showers healing,
as the words of my God
become something tangible,
in the renewing my heart.

GAYLE HEIMBACH BRADSHAW

I FIND HOPE IN YOUR WORD

In all that has happened,
through all the pain I've known,
At times I can't feel you near
and, sometimes then, doubts can grow
But I know deep down inside
that you are always there
Even if I search and still do not see,
I know I've not left Your care

For to deny that in any way
would make your whole Word void
and I've held onto its promise
through all that's been destroyed
I may not understand the pain
or the purpose of it all,
But, Lord, I am here willing,
Prepare me for the call
Whatever it is You desire of me,
That's all I long to be
I catch glimpses, I think, at times,
as You gently set me free

But there is so much that is confusing
How can I be sure of Your voice?
In the cluttered chaos of my mind,
the endless frightening noise
I want so much to make a difference,
The world is so unsure

HOPE THROUGH THE FIRE

I want to make a difference in the despair
I see everywhere I turn.

Lord, I don't want this to be about me.
I don't have to understand
I don't have to have explanations....
I just need You to hold my hand
Use me to bring Your hope to others
who have suffered the frightening freeze,
feeling forever alone
Lord, send springs of life to meet their needs

Make my whole being a testimony
to your endless power and grace,
I pray Your love and mercy,
as I continue to seek your face

GAYLE HEIMBACH BRADSHAW

I CANNOT TAKE MUCH MORE

When I don't want death
but I don't want life,
Where do I go from here?
When I don't want to be stopped
and I don't want help that's near.
When voices hound, and depression rules
and desperation is the name of the game,
the only thing I know for sure
is I have myself to blame.

When you can't even trust yourself
It's a terrifying place to be.
My heart feels bound each way I turn,
I want so much to be free.
But, I feel death in every breath.
I'm not sure why I'm still alive,
but each step that I take
desperation soon arrives.

Moving out from the horror
that kills my heart each night.
It's like being thrown into space
on a timeless, endless flight.
"Fake it 'til you make it"
I've heard so many times before,
But I don't know how to live a lie,
and I cannot take much more

A CHRISTMAS GIFT

Dear God,
It's a funny time
People rushing everywhere
Trees, bulbs, bows
…saying things we should have all year
…the love between us grows.
Lights flicker in majesty
Here on our Christmas trees,
But the lights across the sky
Twinkle as man has never seen.
Your stars, dear Lord, are wondrous,
Full of promise and mystery
Bringing hope of new life
Found in a stable in history.
When your precious son was born
The world changed for eternity
Now we have the honor
To come on bended knee
We come and seek your holy face
Hoping you'll lend ear to our prayers
To the most basic of our cares,
Needs we could speak, but do not dare
It's not the glitter, and the wrapping
That brings us to our knees,
It's the longing for love in our lives
And all we wish we could be
We open our hearts to You, dear God
To the gift of your glorious Son
We hear all he angels of heaven sing

As they look on the Holy One
May we be lights ourselves
To a world in confusion and pain,
To point in awe the King Jesus
For we will never be the same
Make us beacons of your mercy,
To fuel the wings that fly the dove
A shower of grace and forgiveness
Raining down from your heart of love

FIRST CHRISTMAS

The baby lay peaceful and quiet
Sweet Mary brushes hay from the blanket
Shepherds came from afar,
Not knowing yet all that it meant
Could any of them conceive
This was the savior they would one day receive?
A journey for Jesus had just begun,
One that at times would be cold and hard
But to see Him lay there in glory,
Oh what a wonderful start!
If only we had been there,
To touch His face if we dared--
This child so bright and fair
To hold Him in our arms,
Glory of the child with true love amiss
To wrap the blanket tighter 'round,
To offer a sweet, gentle kiss
We may never know
The true glory of that day,
But we know He has changed our hearts and lives
in a victorious, inexplicable way
Let us celebrate the Christ-born child,
with all in our heart and soul
Giving our spirit to His calling,
The most beautiful thing we'll ever know,
As the singing angel voices resound
At that, the very first Christmas of all

MERRY CHRISTMAS, DEAR JESUS

Light pierces the sky
At the glorious break of day
Thinking of You, our Savior
There are no words to say
You—a precious, precious baby
Lay peaceful in Mary's arms
Your eyes shining with new life
Your spirit steady and strong
Could we believe at the sight of Your birth
You would save us from our sins?
…Renew out hurting spirits
bring us new life again
We buy each other gifts at Your birth
But what do we do for You?
Cleanse us by Your mighty power
Make our hearts pure and new
When we look at Christmas Day
It doesn't stop with Your birth
Your passion and sacrifice
The hope you bring to earth
So this is where it all began
In a manger far away
The beginning of eternal life
What an awesome day
From birth, to death, to resurrection
You have given us a new chance
With love, with life, with laughter
You cause our hearts to dance

So, on this special day
Let us take joy in You
To acknowledge the miracle of Your birth
In all that is life and truth

HE IS IN CONTROL

When it hurts because
Things aren't as I planned,
The Lord, my God, takes my hand
He stays there...
And eases the rain
Speaks softly as He says,
"I know your pain
I am your Lord,
In complete control,
I know your heart,
and I know your soul
What happens to you
I must allow,
So let me guide your step,
for I know how
As I heard His words
I broke the chains and stood
"Trust Me My child,
I can work it for good."
Then I realize
As I feel His care,
The void is gone
And His love is there

DO YOU KNOW WHERE YOUR GOD IS?

Do you see Him in the sunrise?
Feel His grace in the breeze?
In the sprinkling morning dew
has your awe yet taken siege?
Does the etched light's mighty splendor
with His love now flood your heart?
Have you the gift of hope
as this new day comes to start?
Are you committed to His ways?
Will you do His will today?
Does your spirit burn within you
as you long the words to say?
Can you feel His mighty mercy
set straight the turmoil of your mind?
Do you limit His power?
Has your confusion left you blind?
Don't you know He is triumphant?
Now make your worry come to an end.
Trust His wisdom to guide--
Let reason finally bend.
Do you know where your God is?
Let His peace this day reign,
this day you've yielded to be His.

PILLOW TEARS

The fiery darts of hell
pierce my heart and mind.
I look to You, Lord
But I don't know what I hope to find.
My body rocks back and forth,
I feel at a total loss.
I don't understand You
or the reality of the Cross.
Why do you look with no emotion?
as I am tormented to the very core.
I love you, Lord,
But I cannot bear much more.
I need some help here, God
Do you feel the anguish in my tears?
Do you see my broken heart?
--the horrid, chilling fears?
I want to understand,
I really do,
but right now all I can do
Is hug this pillow tight
And pretend that it is you

FADED—TO MY FIRST LOVE

Thinking of You
I remember your touch
There were times in the past
when I felt it so much
Now it is just a memory,
faded with my joy and love
Faded as if it never was
I have no pleasant thoughts
at the light of day
No inner stirring
with the words I say
There's no excitement over
things to come
No pleasure in
the things I've done
There's emptiness
and a deep, deep longing,
Any flicker of happiness
long since taken wing

I have struggled a lot about whether or not to include this poem. When looking at my life, it is a vital part of the big picture, and I am putting it in because I think it is one of those defining moments that we all have, that we must surrender to the Lord to find some peace with it.

SILENT SOBS

She shakes with silent sobs.
The imperceptible tick of the clock counts off another minute.
The stagnant terror bitterly chokes her.
Thoughts of rainbows, soft sand castles, and jump ropes are long gone,
Her dreams are of manna in the wilderness.
But the heart-wrenching ghastly moment arrives--
She is alone with him again.
Panic and fear immediately employ indecision--
Fight, resist, and endure more horrific pain?
Or submit to the inevitable.
He says he loves her.
Funny it's the only time he says that.
All supports are totally absent.
Her seven-year-old mind is frozen in terror.
She obediently mops up his needs, as he irascibly destroys hers
and another day passes in their silent, secret world.

I DON'T HAVE TO KNOW WHY

The pains I sometimes feel
can paralyze my heart within
I don't always understand,
Here my confusion begins
Is there something I have done?
Full trust I cannot feign
Faith--
Seems to wax and wane
My emotions and body
are torn, battered, stained
Skeptics ask me to justify...
but I cannot explain
I don't have to know the answers,
I don't doubt that You care
It's belief in Your words of life,
not whether it feels "fair"
Your Peace and Joy
boldly flood my heart,
even when fear and uncertainty
pierce as a glistening knife
The enemy tries to frighten me
--With an outward shine--as power
But a dark, unsettled time
can become the brightest hour
...I don't have to know why
I surrender my all to You,
Heart, mind, spirit, will---
With a clarity that is new

To truly trust,
"Reasoning" has to die
Please melt my logic away,
I don't have to know why

BETWEEN HERE AND THERE

Between here and there
Nowhere
It slips, it slides
It turns, it glides
I am lost inside myself
Please, someone let me out!

Between here and there
Nowhere
Walls . . . Walls everywhere
I can't breathe in here!
It's all I ever run from
Each and every horrid fear
I'm looking at my pen
What keeps me writing on?
Maybe because
All other hope is gone

Between here and there
Nowhere
Caught in my twisting hell
My heart beats triple time
I reach for hands that aren't there
Tell me, which was my crime?
There is no help to come

Between here and there...nowhere

NOON HOUR

Mornings come in glory
as night's darkness fades away
Then, it seems that "high noon"
is the roughest time of day
There is no cover
no where to hide from me
No chance to prepare
all I hope this day will be
The early softness in the air
has turned to blinding sun
I go through my list of strategies
then I start back at one
I do not understand the craze
the confusion and fright...the walls
I can tell myself how far I've come
but it doesn't help at all
Where am I going to?
Why do I live this day?
I listen to suggestions
all anyone has to say
But when can I believe...
when will it take root in my heart?
Sometimes it seems my heart and mind
are a hundred miles apart
I want so much to make it...
want so much to be strong
but the battle has been so difficult...
the war so very long--
I cannot hide from me--

HOPE THROUGH THE FIRE

Does God hate me the way I do?
Does my voice turn Him away?
Does He care about the ache inside...
the wall of fear to even pray?
I cannot escape my own mind
the demons, the confusion...there's no light
Others can see the scorching glow
but I'm deep into the fight
At high noon, all others can see
I feel so very bare
and deep within my soul
I cry out in despair

BRIGHT MORNING STAR

I come now into your presence
Jesus, if you allow
Holy ground surrounds me
Now humbly at Your feet I bow,
So touched by your out-flowing love—
where mercy, love, and holiness meet
Take my heart, dear Lord,
The outpouring of my tears
In reverence to my God
I give the rock of my faults and fears
The rock crumbles around me
Into dust, that blows with the wind
As far as the east is from the west
never to be remembered again
Help me to make a new start
This instant as You hold me near
Sear the guilt and shame
Heal the confusion in my mind
Never again to be the same
I am afraid to move!
I tremble at Your grace
Now You—bearing me up in Your arms
I'm so grateful to see this place
As I go now, to meet my day
In awe, I will never forget
As I gently move forward into Your ways

ROCK-A-BYE BABY

So long Korea
Good-bye Vietnam
We've got a war
right here at home
Fought on U.S. ground,
It' soldiers are the same,
little boys and little girls
meekly bear the shame
A battle of abuse
whose victims far outweigh
the total of casualties
of each war of our day
Their words rejected so one more suffers alone
And those who would care do not see
the inner war which threatens our country
No one wants to say--
No one wants to rock the boat
And when the bell of innocence rings...
It is a silent note

STAIRS

Up and down the stairs
Too fast to see each one
So I close my eyes and run

I'm afraid

Sometimes I long to laugh
Sometimes I long to cry
Caught in a web of doubts
God's "peace train" rumbling by
Where am I?

I'm not really sure how to do this—
Though I have a hundred times
I've slipped away from Your grace
And I'm left still wondering why

Where do I go from here?

What happens now, Lord?
Release me from where I've been
I bare my heart before you....
Can we begin again?

Here we are

On my knees and humble
I place my hand in yours
With passion I surrender
To all You have in store

A NEW MIND

Worn, weary, wounded,
It seemed I'd lost all life
Then, I heard my Jesus say
"Come, my child, arise.
I return your soul to innocence,
the new leaf of my vast love.
There's so much your heart longs to do.
Be patient, there's time enough.
Your reasoning is now reborn--
Revival in the chemistry that has kept you blind.
An eternity in celebration
will be just yours and mine.
You are no longer bound
by confusion's endless need.
I now bring to you more joy and peace
than you ever dared to dream.
I reclaim control of your mind,
and all its frightening tricks.
The jumbled mass of voices
I will destroy with one sweet kiss.
Never again will you search in vain
reaching blindly in darkest night.
Take my hand, and believe, my daughter
Everything's going to be alright."

After years of self-harm and hearing voices that commanded me to act on those feelings, I finally reached a place where I no longer acted on those thoughts and feelings. But, now sometimes it feels like someone else is doing that to me...over and over...like it is happening at that very moment. I have not been able to escape this hellish pain or trying to figure out where the Lord is in these moments. It is still very confusing.

CRINGE

They slice and slice
But no blood flows—
I feel it again and again
Don't know when it begins
Don't know when it ends
It's torture
I cringe with each new slash
I try to check its "reality"
But my mind just moves so fast
Some thoughts I cannot see
When I reach they evade my grasp
I try with all my might
But yet another hour has passed
Time goes on
So frustrating, So frightening
So very much at stake
The pain
Clouds each decision that I make

THE LADDER TO GRACE

Oh, it goes down, quite away I'd say,
Into muck, and mire, and a wash of fallen tears
Light sparks above as I step on the bottom rung.
...Cold, icy...I shriek in fear.
How will I reach God's grace?
My wet, clay-caked boot slips
...My hopes mixed in a pillowcase.
I sling it over my shoulder,
so I climb with one hand alone.
Trying to escape the darkness
with intensity as I've never known.
My efforts get me nowhere.

A pegged rope fell over the wall
and down to the floor of the pit.
I sensed a presence,
it frightened me a bit.
Soon, enormous arms wrapped around my body.
My Lord stood right there in front of me.
He told me how I needn't be afraid.
In awe, I fell to my knees.
He said,
"It's a gift of my love."
He lifted me out of the deep, dark ditch,
Set me on solid ground above.

I can't earn His grace and forgiveness.
I can't do anything good enough.
Our way to the Father

is only through Jesus, His son.
I felt like singing
I shouted to my friends!
"Look where I'm going,
Look where I've been!"

My efforts got me nowhere.
The Lord Almighty gives me new life.
I'm letting go of the past.
My heart has learned to fly.
My efforts got me nowhere.
His grace, after all, was free.

KALAMAZOO

Burnt my thumb
Stupid candle
I've got a guy in Kalamazoo
Spider in my bathroom
Christmas music is getting old already
Tae-Bo
Broken alarm clock, damn thing
Old awards hang around
Hanging around
Hanging around why?
Reminder of some brighter day
A day without roaches
Or age spots on my hands
Archie and Veronica
Dust the pictures
Closest way to my son
Coffee cup from Mexico
Chill in the wind
Chill in my room
Chill in my heart

THE WAY OUT

In a world of secrets,
the silence screams to be heard
The empty caverns etched
by years of the earth's tears
My prayers cut through an eternity's
lack of life and word
Light creeps across each wall and crevice
The emptiness awakes
I have found the way inside
my deepest hurts and hidden fears
I now must patiently press on,
through room after room,
Until I find my way out…
On the other side

SHOUT

Dear God,
I need you,
Like the rose craves the morning dew
Like the field cries for the rain...
A promise of life anew
I love you...
And I'll shout it from the mountain tops!
With all that is within,
Sing it out and never stop!
Like an oasis in endless desert
Mercy flows into sparkling cascades,
Immersing me in Your boundless love
As You joyfully lead the way
Your creation spreads before me,
In its splendor of heavenly hues.
Hold me close to Your heart, dear Jesus,
So I can boldly sing the news!

SACRIFICE

Dear God,
How do I know?
Help me understand.
This drive deep within,
is it brought by Your hand?
I know I can do it... whatever that means.
Something good from the despair
pains my heart has seen.
Am I hearing Your voice?
Your words seems so clear
Though it's sometimes confusing,
I no longer have fear.
Here is my life
body, spirit, mind.
I've committed to You
the words have been signed.
No matter if it hurts,
if it heals others pain.
If it can touch the heart,
if it can ease the rain
Not by mine
but Lord, by Your power.
Help me endure,
bring me more love this hour.
Love enough to give…
love enough to stand.
If this is Your will,
if this is Your plan.
I will not complain

will bear what comes this way.
I want so much to help,
that I know no words to say.
I love you so much, God,
whatever you want of me...
Whatever pleases You,
that's what I want to be.
I'm willing to work hard,
whatever it is You ask.
To encourage others in desperation
with things You've taught me through my past
Please take my hands
as I lift them up to You
A living sacrifice,
to do as You want me to

GAYLE HEIMBACH BRADSHAW

MORNING PEACE

The morning speaks of peace
His grace flooding my soul
Making me finally—finally whole
I feel so very free
Bonds and darkness broken
Sweet, sweet peace
More than I've ever known
God Almighty has touched my life
In ways I can never speak
My mind has turned
In awe and love
I am now complete

FAITH OF A CHILD

He wants us to come to him,
Humbly as a child
Free from ambiguity,
and free from all our pride.
Children gaily singing songs,
They are as hymns to God.
They believe with fervor
in a kind of innocence
most cannot even comprehend--
when they fall off their bike,
they get right back up again.
A child believes until proven wrong
Man will not believe,
what has not been proven,
what he cannot touch or see
Oh, if we could trust as a child
In honest and open prayers,
Instead of what we think to be "fair".
We must come with that child-like trust,
with no doubt of God's words,
and he will lovingly bless us
in ways we've never known.

A TOUCH OF HUMOR

RAP FOR DAVID

Scoop'em
Snag'em
Just gotta have'em
Chasin' a baseball 'round the field
Batter-up, ball's thrown
Ball or strike – ump says he knows
Real man's game – anything goes
Like – yeah – a 150 lb. catcher who likes to sew
Like the wind that blows
Like a dog's cold nose
Like a yard just mowed
Don't even get no dough –
It's the way to go
Ramblin'
Scramblin'
Againin' and againin'
Tryin'
Winin'
Can't stop grinnin'
This is the last innin'

ALL ABOUT TED

Ted was his name,
Golden curls his fame,
and he lived in the house down the street
But early one noon,
he swung too soon,
then he quickly began to retreat
For his ball had smashed through a window,
and fear lent wings to his feet
He'd been told not to play in the yard there,
but its trees gave him shade from the heat
He thought the back route to his neighbor's
the very best route to take,
but his mother hurdled the bushes--
He could not make an escape
His mother was angry and shocked,
but searched for a punishment fair
She sent him straightway to his bedroom,
for solemn confinement there
He had GI Joe and Hot Wheels,
Pooh Bear and Mickey Mouse,
and forbidden secret objects
from every room in the house
He had Sega and Nintendo,
More toys than one could tell
He served out his sentence in laughter,
and it served him quite well

FULL-COURT PRESS

I can't find the words, my Lord,
to say how you fuel my soul
But each time I think I've gotten somewhere
Oh no! You call, "let's go."
A victory won is unspeakable,
I want to rest awhile
Then you nudge me within,
and I break into a smile
I sometimes remind you that my basketball coach
didn't push me quite *this* much
But I know you are even in
The graceful spin of the shooter's touch
There's nothing that is done
That is without your control.
Turn the majestic workings of my heart,
Turn the workings of my soul
Lord, I'm tired, you know,
Today seemed a tortuous walk
And I felt so glad that I made it through
What? This is just the start?
Don't you want some Oreos?
How 'bout a Gatorade or two?
No, Lord, I'll get up…
'Cause I'm thirsty for more of You
Please fill me with Your grace
And ease the "overtime" fear,
And when You need from me a full-court sprint
Give me a swift kick in the rear
I love you so much, Jesus

Put in a good word to Your Father for me
Even if I have go switch to golf,
I want to be what You want me to be

HOW TO STAY AWAKE DURING A POETRY READING

To begin with—never arrive early. See how late you can leave home and still make it to the reading on time. Keep accurate records, and attempt to improve your time.

Once there, listen to the poet reading. Note how his eyebrows match his shoes. Wonder how he would look with his hair combed differently—all six of them.

Pause…and note the poet beside you. Wonder if she likes mustard on French fries.

Wonder if she likes jazz. Listen to the person on the other side of you. Listen to him breathing. Listen to yourself tapping your foot.

Think about the "Mr. Bo-jangles" song you heard on the radio while driving here. Picture Billy Joel singing the song. Picture the poet singing the song to you. Picture yourself getting thrown out of the meeting.

Listen. Listen intently for 5 minutes. Focus on rhythm. Focus on rhyme. Focus on alliteration, and personification.

Jot down a thought for future development. Briefly allow yourself this distraction. Absorb the words. The words. The words.

When you become frustrated, draw stick people. Draw them eating watermelon. Draw them playing soccer. Draw them sitting in a poetry reading.

Oh yeah! Poetry reading. When everyone suddenly stands to their feet, you realize it must be over. As you walk to your car, tell yourself how conscientious you are because you didn't fall asleep. After all, the reading wasn't too bad tonight, it was almost interesting.

TAKE IT ON HOME

THE BRIDGE

Let's build a bridge
from one heart to another,
To the place someone is
From the place you once were
Do you feel their pain?
Do you see their heart?
Help bring understanding
of the one who's been there from the start
Do you remember?
The terror of endless night
The feeling that you had--
Had no way left to fight?
Depression that grips,
Confusion that binds
You know well how God can heal the heart--
How God can heal the mind
Tell of His limitless power--
You are living proof
of how faith and hope can consume
from the very essence of His truth
Let's build a bridge,
from one heart to another,
To the place someone is
From the place you once were

GAYLE HEIMBACH BRADSHAW

I BELIEVE—TO THOSE DEAREST IN MY LIFE

This past year the Lord Jesus
has blessed me beyond words.
The struggle, if words could tell,
many nights and morns,
spent in the pits of hell and hope.
That's part of it,
you know, never giving up hope.
Because there were many who never gave up on
me.
When I called in tears.
When I saw things that were not there,
You comforted me. Pointed me back to what's real.
Because see, it was real to me. As real as life can be.
Changes have come
It may not be "perfect," but it's so, so much better.
A long, long time ago, though it seems like yester-
day,

I remember day, years, decades, have been so long
and hard. But God never gave up
on me, and neither did You.
And, now, over 20 years have passed since this long
ordeal began. I may not be
All what I want and long to be. But, I believe.

And I know the Lord more surely tonight than ever

before.
And I know His love. And I know his peace.
The gift of Jesus brought me to this place.
A place of more joy and peace than I have ever known in my life.
And with God's help, you all brought me here.
And you—you all held my hand, and pulled me along, when I wanted to sit down and cry.

And you—you prayed for me even when it was late, and you were tired, and you didn't feel like praying at all.
And you listened when you didn't feel like it.
When you were having a bad day, and you didn't feel like smiling, you smiled anyway.
You loved me, even when you felt frustrated with me.

You loved me when I wasn't very lovable. Because of you, I can believe.
And I want to say thank you with all my heart.
You have my eternal love and gratitude.

GAYLE HEIMBACH BRADSHAW

FIELDS OF LOVE

I'm running through an open field of daisies
Its fragrance fills my senses
Running as never before
God has pulled down the fences
I roll and laugh and sing
So comforted by the presence of my Lord
The wrapping of death is gone
And my arms and legs—no more cords
He has unleashed my heart
I feel so free and alive!
It's a pool of God's sweet love
I think I'll jump and dive—dive right in!

LaVergne, TN USA
04 November 2009
163105LV00001B/70/P